DESIGNING WITH

SPIRITUALITY

The Creative Touch

DESIGNING WITH
SPIRITUALITY

The Creative Touch

Carol Soucek King, MFA, PhD

PBC International
     incorporated

distributor to the book trade in the united states and canada
Rizzoli International Publications Inc., through St. Martin's Press
175 fifth avenue   new york   new york   10010

all other distribution
PBC International Incorporated
one school street   glen cove   new york   11542

for a free catalog
PBC International Incorporated
one school street   glen cove   new york   11542
call toll free   1 800 527 2826
within new york state   516 676 2727
facsimile   516 676 2738
e-mail   pbcintl@aol.com

library of congress cataloging-in-publication data available

ISBN 0-86636-691-1

CAVEAT—Information in this text is believed accurate, and will pose no problem for
the student or casual reader. However, the author was often constrained by information contained in signed release forms, information that could have been in error or
not included at all. Any misinformation (or lack of information) is the result of failure
in these attestations. The author has done whatever is possible to insure accuracy.

10 9 8 7 6 5 4 3 2 1   Printed in Hong Kong

To spirituality at home, and
being at home with spirituality!

DESIGNING
WITH

SPIRIT

UALITY

Sorry to repeat myself, but in the last sentence of a book titled A Philosophy of Interior Design, I wrote that interiors constitute "our most personal art." Carol Soucek King, I'm glad to see, seems to share the same view, for the admirable series of books Dr. King has planned promises to focus on just those aspects of interior design that make it personal.

The grand concept is not to be neglected, of course. Like any other art, interior design depends for its success on the encompassing vision that relates its many elements in a meaningful whole. But such vision, in interiors, becomes manifest and comprehensible through the medium of myriad details with which we are in intimate contact: the feel of a drawer-pull, the profile of a cornice, the polish and grain of wood, the "hand" of fabric.

This contact involves all our senses. We see our interiors, certainly, but we also smell the materials in them, we hear their acoustic properties, we brush up against their walls, step on their floors, open their case-goods, sit on their chairs. More than any other, interior design is the art we use. In that sense, it is not only our most personal art, but also the one most responsible for our well-being. In the context of increasingly brutalized urban environments, this is increasingly true and increasingly important. Interior design is often our refuge.

It is therefore a very welcome prospect that Dr. King is turning her experienced editorial eye to the details and materials on which the art of interior design depends. I'm sure we will all benefit from her discoveries.

Stanley Abercrombe, FAIA
Vice President, Editorial Director
INTERIOR DESIGN

Welcome to Designing with Spirituality, the sixth book in "The Creative Touch" series published by PBC International Incorporated. Similar to Designing with Tile, Stone & Brick, Designing with Wood, Designing with Glass, Designing with Fabric and Designing with Light, this volume is also devoted to one aspect of residential interiors. Yet this volume's purpose is to show how all those previous materials are transformed with form, scale, color and line to express the individual's connection to the essence of life.

Twenty years ago a book devoted to the spirituality of design would have found its way into the publisher's round file before the author could finish praying. Today, however, it is well known that most people believe in the sacredness of personal space as a refuge from an overly hectic world, if not for more mystical reasons. Yet the preponderance of the architects and designers I know, as well as their clients, are deeply interested in the more deeply spiritual perspective and using design to express it in the home.

Each individual interviewed and each project shown serve as testament to the belief that good design is much more than skin deep. While comforting and protective, they celebrate the idea of home as heightened awareness of the connection of the everyday life to the spiritual.

Enjoy!

Carol Soucek King

introduction

I feel that, as designers, architects and artists, our gifts come from God. In trying to make the world a better place, we are but vehicles. We have been given certain gifts. The arts may be a business but the gift is something divine.

Too many times we design for what we think the client wants. Instead, we should design from a philosophy and a point of view —like Brancusi, the sculptor who had a singular vision. He did it by going into his studio and staying with his view of the world. By staying with your own vision, by digging deeper into your own intuition, you are more likely to tap into a spirit that is not only your own individual voice but one that speaks more to others as well. To me, that is spiritual.

It is that spiritual sense of connectedness to the universal that we should bring to the home. For the home is our sanctuary, the place where we terminate each day and originate the next. It is where we connect with loved ones and friends. Everything about it represents ritual, a ritual that is part of everyday life.

Design is not transactional. It's transformational. It transforms people's lives. It's not about what we have. It's about the evolution of the human spirit.

I feel that we don't give enough credit to the source of all inspiration—the divine—and am pleased that Carol Soucek King's book opens this up for contemplation.

Barbara Barry

meditative havens

magical
power

Los Angeles
California

photography by
Tom Bonner

In designing his own residence, architect **Jeffrey Daniels** has bridged found qualities of current culture with a sense of the uncanny. He believes in using architecture as a process to make magic.

"Unfortunately, the idea of magic has too often been co-opted by the relentless 'Disney-izing' of theme parks around the world, where everything is reduced to storybook nostalgia," he says. "But in primitive animistic cultures, which revered the transformative power of a shaman, certain objects were believed to have the power to affect the quality of people's lives. Bringing this attitude to the design of a house is a tentative step to try and recapture some of this transformative power and to restore a sense of uncanny magic in the making of architecture."

The tight dimensional restrictions of the 25-foot by 100-foot site led to a design that is compact, rectilinear and tall. Containing 1,700 square feet of living space, the house includes two bedrooms, a mezzanine office/ guest room and three baths.

The architecture attempts to dramatize the inevitable box-like shape that evolved from maximizing the available space. The upper living level is set off from the lower base by a contrasting copper cladding and a five-degree shift in geometry. Facing the rear yard, a projecting wood trellis extends the space defined by the house into the surrounding greenery. On the interior, the primary living spaces are made as open as possible to counter the compactness of the building's overall footprint.

Conceived as a modest utilitarian dwelling, this house also serves as a place for quiet reflection—reinforced by the use of natural materials throughout.

The base of the exterior is covered in a smooth terra-cotta stucco, its hue referring to the ground of the area's granite hills. The upper portion is clad with patinated copper, its green color echoing the surrounding landscape. ✧ The interior's openness recalls the loft the architect might have called home had he remained in New York. Elements that divide areas, such as the slatted screen that forms a guardrail for the stair and the rusted-steel handrail, reveal the space beyond. ✧ The kitchen's cherry wood cabinetry continues the home's prevailing reverence for nature. The architect designed the dining chairs and stained them a muted green that continues the subdued but noticeable Japanese influence in his other wood detailing.

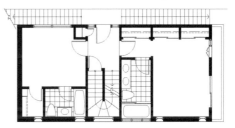

first floor

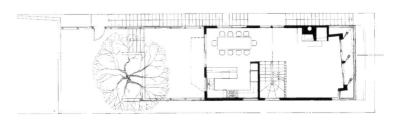

second floor

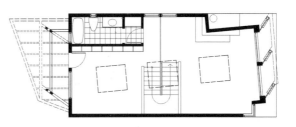

mezzanine

"I agree with André Malraux—the next one hundred years will be the century of spirituality," says textile designer **Pietro Seminelli**. In his own residence and studio, a former cabinetmaker's shop in a wood structure in the heart of Paris, that century seems to have arrived ahead of schedule.

With each piece of furniture, each carefully selected and placed object, Seminelli has orchestrated a place that radiates calm. His folded fabric creations are draped throughout the interior, modulating the flow of light in deft and magical ways.

Seminelli compares his work to folding ideas into souls. It is an apt description. Using only natural materials—Manila hemp, ramie (nettle), linen, cotton, silk, abaca (banana fiber), pineapple fiber, paper and silk—he combines age-old techniques, inspired by Japanese origami, with new ones to weave a seamless, ethereal world.

"My creations have been directly influenced by this studio's feeling," he says. "It gets so much light during the day that it constantly inspires me to create new ways to filter light."

The plis, or folds, with which Seminelli transforms fabrics, work like stained glass. Their geometries and subtle colors make the light uniquely palpable. In front of windows, across skylights or simply dividing spaces, the folded textiles cast a meditative spell.

"This was my quest," explains the designer. "I believe the place where we live is the image of our 'inner house'. It acts as a matrix for our own monde intérieur. For those who can read them, our homes reflect our inner images in their folds."

home as
"inner house"

Paris
France

photography by
Cecile & Stefano Poli

The designer enjoys rare pieces for their historical interest, their visual impact and their materials. For example, his 1930s mahogany chest of drawers from the Philippines conveys the influence of the Japanese. ❖ A skylight provides an ideal showcase for hue and weave while creating a subdued light within the sleeping area. Throughout, the open space can be changed via a series of sliding panels depending on mood or need. ❖ Only natural materials are used throughout, not only in the fabrics but also the furniture. The colors are also derived from natural vegetal dyes and are subdued in tone, providing a sense of quiet thoughtfulness.

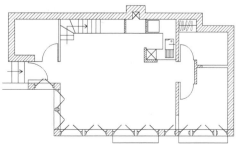

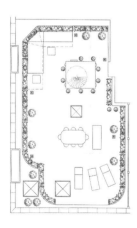

urban oasis

Metropolitan
New York

photography by
Hugo A. Rojas

Imagine: Living in the midst of eight million people and having your own roof court oasis just to meditate in private. What could be more wonderful than a garden in the air when the pace and pressures of city life seem relentless?

Architect **Geoffrey Scott** and his clients have turned that fantasy into reality. This 986-square-foot courtyard atop a landmark, Stanford White-designed building adds another level to the clients' penthouse, providing an outdoor room dedicated to the pursuit of relaxation. Daybeds and a sunshade structure offer rest and relaxation. Areas for dining and gathering flow in a harmonious plan. A garden with trees, green plants and flowers establishes a sense of enclosure.

Scott faced numerous challenges to realizing the design: he was prohibited from penetrating the roof structure or attaching anything to the building. Moreover, the roof had no elevator access, just a narrow stair. As a solution, Scott devised a deck with a support system inspired by a spider's legs.

A major premise of Scott's design was that the roof court's several areas be adaptable. Thus the terrace, which appears as a parquet deck, is actually a modular grid that can be rearranged. Planters serving as walls of greenery are movable, as are all other furnishings, lighting and pots. New outdoor rooms can be created at will.

The result is a space where the only forces apparently at work are natural ones: air, water, sky, clouds, plants.

An aerial view shows the relationship of the roof court's various areas, including the designer's use of the pyramidal skylights as garden sculpture. Trex was chosen for the parquet deck surface, as it is an environmentally correct material as well as feels barefoot-comfortable and will not splinter. ◇ By evening, night lighting turns the roof top into an illuminated oasis amid the sparkling city skyline.

Architect/designer **Sig Bergamin** brings the feeling of exotic adventure to everything he designs, including small com missions such as this window display. Whether highlighting turn-of-the century nostalgia at a Long Island residence, or the wild countryside of his native Brazil, Bergamin always demands that the imagination take flight.

Here, his idea was to create a window for Artefacto, a store in the heart of São Paulo that specializes in home furniture. The design emphasizes materials such as wicker and bamboo—connecting Brazil's natural pursuits as they relate to this city's people today.

"The concept," says Bergamin, "was to simulate a small three-room home (living, dining, bedroom) that would both explore the diversity of ethnic materials and also create a peaceful, relaxing atmosphere. I wanted to express the kind of environment that would appeal not only to people's eyes but also stimulate their senses and appeal to their souls."

Bergamin's combination of primarily Asian elements creates a decidedly Zen-like atmosphere, a mystical aura by which Bergamin intentionally suggests the idea that decoration can have a spiritual value.

"It seems that all over the world this is the language of the 1990s. The house remains one of the few places where we can reenergize ourselves after a long and stressful day. It's our cozy nest in which to take refuge. So, to me, that is in tune with the concept of spirituality in decoration. We need for it to provide us with much more than a roof over our heads. We need for it to restore our mind and our emotions. We need a place where we can dream."

mystical
aura

São Paulo
Brazil

photography by
Tuca Reinés

Fragments of a 19th-century Chinese wooden screen serve as backdrop for dinner served in blue-and-white porcelain on a Chinese elm wood table. ❖ A firey contrast to the room's subdued, meditative atmosphere is brought by the deep-red lacquered finish of a 19th-century Chinese armoire brings. ❖ The walls have been sponged with hues of blue and cream, evoking a feeling of soaring in the clouds or on the wings of dreams. Antique prints and fragments of ancient buildings suggest the need to contemplate man's cultural roots. ❖ A mosquito net of Egyptian cotton turns an antique Chinese bed, covered in silk from India, into a cozy retreat.

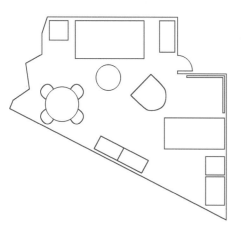

enlightened
structure

Sheffield
Massachusetts

photography by
Michael Janeczek

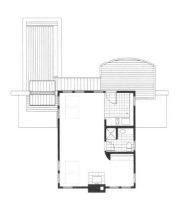

"To be a soulful, sensual place...its spirituality corresponding to the root of the word, which means simply 'to breathe'." That was architect **Tom Barrie's** aim for the small studio he designed for artists Steven Rost and Andrea Eis, and their two children.

Located in the lake-dotted, mountainous terrain of the Berkshires, the 600-square-foot structure encompasses a studio and dark room on the first floor and living and sleeping spaces on the second.

A 40-foot-long, 10-foot-high concrete block wall aligns the house to its cardinal points and frames views of mountain and lake. The kitchen faces the morning sun, and the screened porch faces the lake. The living room faces the mid-summer sunrise as well as an opening in the concrete wall that, like the "borrowed landscape" of traditional Zen gardens, precisely frames the mountain view.

Inside and out, ordinary materials are used straightforwardly: a galvanized steel roof; exposed concrete block walls; Western red cedar siding applied with the rough, re-sawn side exposed. The pattern of panels and stainless steel screws expresses the handiwork of the builder. Cedar decks and stairs feature similarly exposed attachments, as do conduit deck railings, plywood flooring attached with galvanized steel screws, and the galvanized conduit used for ladder rungs.

The totality expresses architecture's fundamental act—the mediation between earth and sky. The wall is firmly grounded in earth. The roof reflects the sky. The studio symbolizes human experience caught between earth and heaven.

"Spiritual architecture is enlightening...leading one to a deeper connection with the world," says Barrie. "The aim of this artists' retreat was for it to become a threshold to an expanded position in the universe."

The studio, clad in rough-sawn western red cedar, is capped by a shiny galvanized steel roof. A 40-foot-long concrete block wall marks the studio and transforms the site. It also serves as a giant sundial, its sides casting no shadow at solar noon.

The atmosphere of complete serenity pervades one's entire being when arriving at Villa Melati, the Balinese retreat that Hong Kong-based architect **Martin Smyth** designed for himself and his wife, Yajaira. The tranquilizing of the mind, and hence the body, is immediate.

The air—clean and clear but carrying the scents of spices, herbs and coconut cooking oil—permeates the consciousness. So, too, do the freshness of the semi-tropical vegetation and the aroma of the ubiquitous burning incense.

The route to the house proceeds through the terraced and landscaped gardens via a stepped path of 93 stone risers with seven landings en route. Smyth has organized a ceremonial entry that continues to lead ever deeper into the site past garlands of vines, golden bamboo groves and cascading pools. Once the destination is reached, the layering of unusual, yet instantly comforting, sights and pleasures continue inside a series of serene enclosures. Constructed almost entirely of indigenous materials—local stones and woods, grass roofs supported on bamboo rafters—the villa harmonizes with its surroundings as well as any man-made intrusion possibly could.

Simplicity is the essence, proportion the byword. Flexibility is another partner in this paradise, with spaces able to close or open depending on mood and weather.

As Smyth continues to discover, spending time here is a transporting experience. "One's concerns fall away and lose their relevance. You become aware of the most basic—yet truly the most sophisticated—aspects of the elements that surround and support our lives on this planet."

bliss in bali

Kedewatan
Bali, Indonesia

photography by
Charis Mundy

Throughout, open and closed spaces play off one another, casting shadows on the locally made clay tile. ◇ The pool's natural green slate lining reflects a translucent green under lights at night. ◇ In the master bedroom, local tile is interspersed with strips of wood to create diagonals in harmony with the roof. Walls of Javanese green slate and beach stones surrounding a wood strip floor turn a bathroom into an open mini-garden.

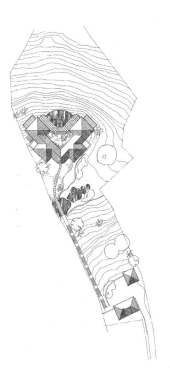

**sense
of calm**

Los Angeles
California

photography by
© David Glomb

A palpable calm pervades Dr. Scott Lander's three-story Los Angeles townhouse. Lander, a chiropractor who occasionally sees patients at his residence, requires that kind of harmonious environment in both his personal life and his professional pursuits. Thus it's no wonder that the finely honed sensibilities of designer Brad Blair's work appeal to him: sparely placed Asian collectibles; elegant and comfortable upholstery; a sophisticated color palette of cappuccino, bamboo, cane, mud, honey and seagrass interrupted with expanses of white; the quiet cadence of a working fountain in a courtyard lily pond.

Blair, a designer and importer through his firm Lotus Antiquities, places far more than a monetary value on Eastern antiques: "Very few cultures have blended function and form so well, with no pretense or ego in the construction and design. I am drawn to their energy. I am romanced by their having been possessed by countless others, leaving their indelible marks—sometimes in obvious ways, such as wear and patina. But always, especially with the very old pieces, there exists a measurable resonant energy. I say measurable as it has been demonstrated to me, with a device which measures magnetic field."

Blair always allows the architecture, in this case the grand idiom of Hollywood's glamorous 1920s, to predominate. At the Lander house, Blair achieved this by removing vestiges of past remodeling mistakes, such as awkward and useless breaks in walls. The splendidly soaring sloped ceilings remain as odes for inspiration.

Otherwise, the interiors are emphatically low and horizontal—invitations to stillness and peace.

Accessible through a tall paneled door painted dark green, the courtyard centers on a birdbath, a reminder that water is the source of all living things. The fir floor is finished with a wash of lavender to ease tension and discipline in the dining area. French doors open into a private, vine-covered patio. ❖ Stairs leading to the adjusting room and bedroom above provide an uncluttered view of the first floor and patio beyond. ❖ In the bedrooms, the sight level was brought down to a more human scale by covering wardrobes with vintage Japanese sliding reed doors, yoshido. Cove light troughs are covered with custom, flush mounted, metal framed paper shades. An antique two-part kimono chest, tansu, was configured horizontally instead of stacked. Antique Japanese linen floor pillows, zabuton, further support the low, horizontal aesthetic.

first floor

second floor

third floor

Interior designer **Sandra Nunnerley** has spent much of her life trekking the globe in search of knowledge and enlightenment. The fascinating mementoes she has collected along the way weave an almost Jungian tapestry of her inner journey.

There is no way the Asian/European/South American mix in her Sutton Place apartment could be construed as merely material. The console—draped with Buddha fabric from Lhasa and arranged with the five positions of Buddha as well as the traditional Buddhist offering of fruit—looks more like an altar. And it is.

"I have studied Buddhism, and it continues to be my outlook on life," says Nunnerley in the lovely lilt acquired during a childhood in New Zealand and Australia. "If I didn't meditate every morning, I couldn't keep the rest of it together."

But Nunnerley is a master at keeping her life intact. When not designing, she spends it traveling. "I've lived all over the world, including Paris and New York. And, of course, growing up where I did, the Asian world is at your fingertips. I also find South America very spiritual. I find Africa fascinating. And I still go back to Tibet and Nepal. All these places become part of me."

That is why, when ethnic art and artifacts are seen in Nunnerley's own home, they seem part of her as well. Set against a highly textural background of loosely-woven linen, silk damask and ebonized wood floor, the objects represent the deeply etched markings of her own personal map.

As multi-dimensional as the collection is, it feels quieting, like a temple for meditation. And it is.

personal
quest

New York City
New York

photography by
Jaime Ardiles-Arces
Paul Hyman

Nunnerley's altar is grounded on the Buddha fabric she found in Lhasa, Tibet. ❖ In the dining room, a silver mirror from Peru reflects Nunnerley's interest in the Incas' masterful work in silver and gold, which continues to this day. ❖ Each object has a very special meaning to me," says Nunnerley of her collection, including a feathered headdress she acquired while in the Amazon, two Korean chests, 18th-century drawings of candelabra by an Italian draftsman and French Empire candlesticks.

sequestered tranquility

Matsumoto
Nagano Prefecture
Japan

photography by
Shiro Nakane

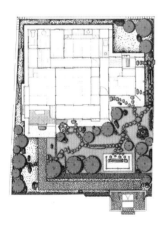

Tranquility pervades the atmosphere as soon as one leaves the contemporary bustle of the ancient castle town of Matsumoto and steps within the roofed walls and bamboo fences to the teahouse and garden within. The owners' main house is just steps away, yet they wanted to pursue their deep study of the wabi-cha tea ceremony in an appropriate atmosphere. Without visual interruption they could emphasize life's essentials and eschew the frivolous.

"The wabi-cha tea ceremony has the same meaning as the religious practice of Zen Buddhism, and using and maintaining the tea garden itself empowers the life of the owners and their guests," says landscape architect **Shiro Nakane**.

The idea is to live in harmony with all the elements of the universe. The wabi-cha tea garden is a copy of nature, with every tree and plant providing a means to interchange with nature. The daily rituals of cleansing and watering the tea garden and preparing tea within the meditative serenity of the teahouse are Zen practices in the pursuit of excellence, wisdom and understanding.

Although designed in the form of a traditional tea garden, this garden includes some subtle variations—the feeling of a long approach despite the site's limited size and the selection of trees that change color in autumn. Above all, a tea garden should have some original contrivance: Nakane planned a drain chiriana under the eaves to collect used water, since Nagano's heavy snowfalls preclude the use of the stone water basin tsukubai during the winter. This kind of contrivance, based on an old document, is becoming rare today.

Only natural materials are used for the wabi-cha teahouse, reflecting the idea of living in subdued simplicity to achieve philosophical refinement. Tea gardens in general have no trees with brilliant flowers and fragrance in order to let those notes of hospitality be expressed through arranged flowers and incense inside. Yet Nakane did plant trees such as Japanese maple, Euonymum alatus and Enkianthus perulatus, which change color in the autumn. Traditional stone lanterns further the feeling of being faraway from modern invention and closer to the quest for age-old wisdom. As in the area leading to the roofed waiting bench koshikake-machiai, every stone is considered a treasure, its placement an aesthetic decision requiring meditation as well as skill.

No matter that the location is New York City. Whenever the owners of this urbane residence return from their constant worldwide travels, they never cease to be amazed that their favorite destination is actually home—the double townhouse duplex with a private Bonsai garden. As orchestrated by interior designer **Glenn Lawson**, the sense of serenity is nothing short of remarkable.

Two complete apartments were combined to create one flowing environment. Two stairways, one east and one west, provide the option for circular movement throughout the house. One can ascend from the entry foyer and descend near the media room, or vice versa. What truly emphasizes the flow of space with a breezy gracefulness is the way Lawson has harmonized color, pattern and form inside with the natural elements of the garden, which can be seen from every room.

The living level interprets a range of earth and water tones. The upper level, where natural illumination is even more abundant, features a palette that lightens and becomes more ethereal. Upstairs and down, the various circular patterns and shapes conveyed through a wealth of natural materials echo the home's gently sweeping rhythm.

As a dramatic contrast, the entrance emphasizes the geometric quality of the floating, backless steps that rise over an Escher-inspired painted floor. The floor's three-dimensional appearance creates an illusion of endless layers of space. Lawson favors this surreal device and employs it once again with his placement of the owners' collection of Oriental figures in period costumes. Whether sitting on tables or peeking down from some bookshelf's topmost reaches, they further blur the line between reality and dream.

astonishing
solitude

New York City
New York

photography by
© Wade Zimmerman

The media room, which combines the library's printed matter with an audio-visual system, seems in fact untouched by today's fast-paced world. With the planting of 2,000 bulbs, some exquisite invention of nature is in constant, visible bloom. ◈ At the entry, Lawson juxtaposed an antique European tapestry with a contemporary floating staircase and an Escher-inspired floor painted to look three-dimensional. ◈ A lighter, cloud-like palette of the fabrics combined with Impressionist and Post-Impressionist paintings reflect the master bedroom's second floor location and its proximity to the sky. The antique Chinese fourposter bed is treated simply, with pagoda sheers on either side.

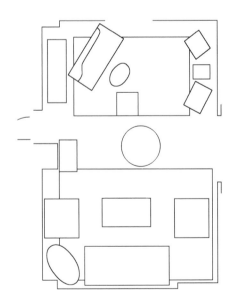

ordered enchantments

positive
energy

Santa Monica
California

photography by
Toshi Yoshimi
Photography
courtesy of
Interior Design
magazine

Architect **J. Frank Fitzgibbons** has designed a house that gathers its energy from the garden, its spiritual center. The joyful embrace of articulated terraces filled with flowers, water elements, hard surface and lawn, is reflected inside. The interior's different ground floor levels, provocative geometries, exuberant hues and varying textures stimulate the mind. A balanced asymmetry provides a provocative yet harmonious environment where the spirit can flourish like a well-tended landscape.

"The idea," says Fitzgibbons, "was to derive the largest sunny and protected garden possible on a long, narrow, slightly sloping lot. Private family spaces form a wall lining the north edge. Public entertaining spaces enclose the west street frontage, thus providing shade to the garden from the afternoon heat."

Changes in floor level differentiate the areas on the ground floor and echo the gentle steps of the exterior garden. In the same way, progressively lowered ceiling heights reflect the emotional progression as one moves from public to private spaces.

Color, the most important aesthetic element of Fitzgibbon's design, is key. Public areas are framed by smooth yellow stucco; family areas are identified by a textured white finish. A circular stair tower at the intersection of the house's two wings is an eye-popping magenta, a hue repeated in the joints interlacing all the elevations and reflecting the interdependency of the parts.

The effect is that of a Modernist painting, one infused with a spirit more often attributed to the Impressionists, an apt analogy. Fitzgibbons, trained as a painter and sculptor as well as an architect, considers that one of the major problems with contemporary architecture is that it ignores the value of layering space, color and light.

Steps up to the dining room at left and steps down to the living room at right echo and celebrate the natural flow of land on this site. Colorful effusions demarcate the dining area, the entry and the living room. The bridge above leads to the mezzanine's library. Spaces throughout reflect the multiple layers which fashion life's experiences. According to Fitzgibbons, "Our environments must be more than just objects in space."

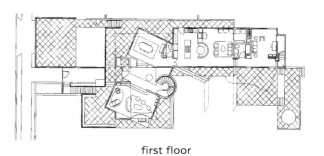

first floor

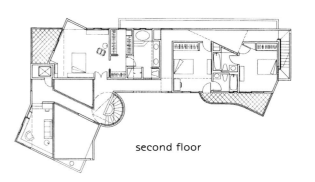

second floor

The architecture of **Ricardo Legorreta** keeps reminding us that there is nothing more magnificent than simplicity. In the getaway home Legorreta designed for a busy family in Mexico's Valle de Bravo, the enormity of his vision echoes through its peaceful, private reaches. Arrival proceeds along an entry path through a lemon orchard and culminates in a motor court of labyrinth-patterned stones: one does not just park the car—one sheds it along with all other urban toxins.

Located on a five-acre site that overlooks both a golf course and the mountains that are a national reserve, the house faces south, thereby maximizing the view and the flow of natural light. Walls of different heights save the impact of the panorama for the view from the interior. The journey through the house is one of discovery. Each space becomes apparent one at a time. Even the exterior landscape slowly reveals itself through the windows. The owners say they have found here the pleasures of life—walking, mystery and discovery. Then, too, the sound of water is a constant; water cascades from the entry patio down steps to an expansive pool lined with river stones. Its music permeates every space with an elevated, soft but lively spirit.

The interiors were designed by Ricardo Legorreta together with his son Victor, an architect who is an associate in his father's firm. Many pieces of the furniture were designed especially for the house, taking advantage of the extraordinary craftsmanship available in Mexico.

Not surprisingly, after spending numerous weekends here, the clients decided that Legorreta Arquitectos should design them another house in the city so they will be able to experience these same feelings daily.

magnificent
simplicity

Valle de Bravo
Mexico

photography by
Lourdes Legorreta

The front doors open to a vaulted hall that runs along the living room through the bedroom wing. The living space, located at the midpoint of the longitudinal axis, is emphasized with an inclined roof. Using stone, bronze and woods, the architect took advantage of the fine local craftsmanship in designing not only furniture but all custom detailing. ❖ Private spaces are separated into two levels, with the master bedroom on the second level. Furniture and candles turn the bathroom into a place to linger.

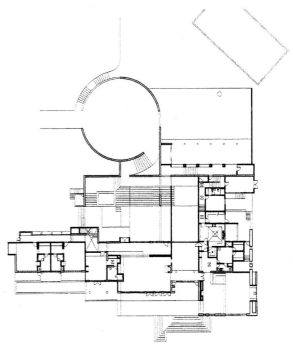

Every time I move, I find I need less," says interior designer **Geoffrey N. Bradfield**. His recent change of residence gave him the ideal opportunity to practice this minimalist principle.

Viewing his new apartment's pristine emptiness as a blank canvas, Bradfield edited and pared down his possessions. Compared to the relative crowdedness of his previous residence, this new, spare interior contains only a few items that commingle with its Zen-like purity.

What was invited to accompany him to this resolutely minimalist environment is a disparate, but spiritually cohesive, collection of art. Simplicity, perhaps, is the common binding thread. Kenneth Noland's disciplined and serenely clean-lined canvases; Gwynn Murrill's fluid feline; the fine collection of African headrests, ebony outlines poised against stark white shelving like characters from some untranslatable language. Each suggests hidden mysteries and concealed meanings worthy of contemplation.

"It's intriguing to think of the Masai warriors and tribal princes who have taken their ease sleeping on these exquisitely carved rests...planning battle strategy...dreaming dreams," notes Bradfield.

Each piece of furniture is treated as a work of art. Its placement identifies it as something worthy of note. Its position evokes a sense of inherent life far beyond that of an inanimate object.

What Bradfield likes best about orchestrating such mesmerizing juxtapositions in his sea of calm is the interior's resultant monastic aura. "There is something to be said for the need of the attendant solitude that I think accompanies the creative process," he says.

monastic
solitude

New York City
New York

photography by
© 98 Durston Saylor

Only two notes of color are allowed to punctuate the sea of neutral calm. Shelf lighting accentuates the dramatic display of African headrests. The ceiling's perimeter is highlighted to provide visual lift and extend the sense of spaciousness. ◇ Amid the bedroom's otherwise meditative serenity, an exotically figured screen is prominently placed and backlit.

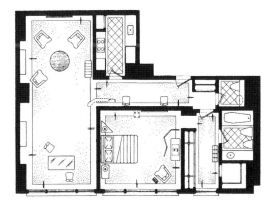

The nature that inspires Californians also challenges their fortitude in the face of possible disasters. When the Jacobson family decided to build on the footprint of a house that had burned in the 1991 Painted Cave firestorm, they embraced the surrounding natural beauty while respecting the volatility of the environment.

Working with **Robin Donaldson** and **Russell Shubin** of Shubin + Donaldson Architects, the clients sought a new structure that would use only natural materials—preferably native ones—particularly those that might withstand the wildfires that periodically storm through the canyon.

Given a budget of $100 per square foot, the architects proposed the use of modest materials in creative ways. Fire-resistant cement board, steel and timber form the exterior walls of a house composed of simple, rectangular elements with sloping roof lines, a design influenced by a nearby community of turn-of-the-century wood fishing cabins.

Despite its relatively small size of 2,000-square feet, the result—a three-story, downslope-facing structure—creates the impression of a large compound. Sage-colored siding and plaster tinted to look like ochre-hued sandstone blend into the indigenous stone and brush. A V-shaped chimney top makes an overt nod to the topography of the canyon.

The main living area of the residence opens out onto a timber deck. The view looks south down the valley to the ocean, and facilitates the indoor/outdoor lifestyle that drew this family to honoring the spirit of California's landscape in the first place.

new
waves
west

Santa Barbara
California

photography by
Assassi Productions

Hues of the exterior's wood siding and plaster echo the surrounding California landscape. Nestled in a coastal mountain valley overlooking the Pacific Ocean, the house design pays tribute to nature. The main living area opens onto a timber deck that overlooks the ocean. Large picture windows provide views to the north. ❖ The owner's request to incorporate native materials to the extent possible inspired the use of stone taken from the site for the fireplace surround Marmoleum, an environmentally safe product made from rubber trees, is used for flooring throughout.

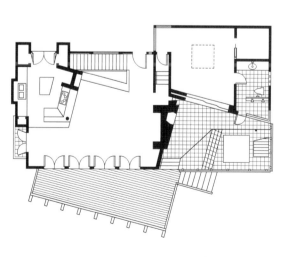

less but
better

Phoenix
Arizona

photography by
© Mark Boisclair

When designers **Eric** and **Dorothy Bron** decided to leave their sprawling ranch-style home, they realized that what they wanted was not more but less.

"Our children are grown. We have everything we need. We're more interested in paring down," says Dorothy. "We want to utilize the space we have, not have more space than we need."

Their selection of an existing 2,700-square-foot home on a small but protected lot was perfect: minimal and urbane, with views of the mountains and city, but still as private as can be.

As designers, the Brons have access to sophisticated and elegant materials. Yet, they felt that, for themselves, the innovative use of simple materials would be more satisfying. Floors were stripped to concrete in most areas. Walls were removed to open up spaces between rooms. Busy wall coverings were removed or painted over with off-the-shelf glossy paint in hues that nourish the Brons' emotional well-being. Assisting in the remodel was architect **Walter Bendix Nelson, Jr.**, who created north-facing windows to welcome the desert's embracing light and extend the view to the mountains. Shaman **Taffy Lanser** advised on the spiritual aspect of occupying this space.

One of the major challenges in downsizing one's home is finding room for beloved furnishings acquired through the years. So it was with the Brons and their prized collection of early-20th-century Monterey furnishings, particularly because their personal favorite style is modern. Still, since many of these period possessions are family heirlooms, in the end the Brons worked out a marriage of Old West and Modern that reflects their approach to the true essence of life. And it works!

A row of windows brings additional light into the living room. while the collection of vintage Monterey furniture contrasts treasured gifts with the Brons' more Modernist leanings. ❖ The master bedroom contains a Coromandel screen and a black lacquer cabinet that Eric Bron designed to house television, tapes and books. The Brons' passion for art includes a sculpture by Larry Yanez, left, a work by Suzanne Klotz, right, and a glass bust by Dan Dailey.

Although the budget for this guesthouse designed by architects **Regina Pizzinini** and **Leon Luxemburg** was small, the result is proof that quality architecture, spaces and experience depend not on money but on ideas.

The idea of building a separate building just for your guests is an indication of generous personalities, so just in planning it, Roger and Julie Corman already set in motion a feeling of harmonious sharing. This structure is undeniably integrated with its site. All but the roofscape is obscured from above. The walls start gently at the crest of a hill. As they descend, they emerge in a structure that opens to the view beyond.

"You walk down away from everyone else. All you see is nature. There is nothing else but sycamores, pittosporum and eucalyptus trees swaying in the breeze," Pizzinini says. "Your back is protected by the hill. The front is open for your thoughts, your dreams, new ideas. Nothing disturbs these thoughts. The undisturbed surroundings ask for them."

The house itself divides neatly into two parts. One side accommodates a bathroom and kitchen; the other side is a library where skylights let you experience the sun's movement throughout the day.

This rejuvenating, constantly beckoning space has never had a specific label. It has been used as a painting studio, a party room for children, an extension for guests to use as their living room or additional sleeping facility. Very often, it has served as an empty space for meditation, it also doubles as the pool house.

Regardless of its function, nothing changes. This is a place that celebrates life as a recreation of the mind.

recreation
of the mind

Santa Monica
California

photography by
Dominique Vorillon

This guesthouse serves as a retreat for the Corman's almost as often as for guests. The dining area connects to the library opening onto a terrace and to the outdoors. The sofabed in the dining area easily converts the space into sleeping quarters. Inviting meditation is the classic modern chair by Charles Eames and the drawing is by Stephen Sidelinger.

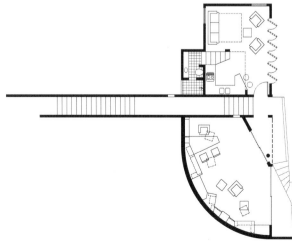

poetry for the soul

Central Florida

photography by
Everert & Soulé
Orlando

Created for two professional designers who travel extensively throughout the Orient, this lakeside home combines the couple's artistic sensibilities. It blends Asian art and artifacts with their own Southeastern U.S. traditions into a peaceful retreat.

Joan and Roland DesCombes, the principals of Architectural Artworks, have long believed that architecture speaks as poetry to the soul. To them, this signifies an inextricable link between architecture and site: the integration of design with nature means that no part of anything is of greater value than its value as an integral part of the whole. The practical is not one thing, the beautiful another.

They float roof lines to the horizon with ribbons of windows, approximating the rising and setting of the sun. They create abstract patterns with inner geometries, describing a discernible organic pattern of all things in nature. To them, the reality of a building is its space within and without, as it is here.

Says Roland DesCombes, "Space must be a free horizontal flow through the fabric of the structure with cascades of light all along the perimeters. Creating this combination allows the occupant the freedom to feel at one with the structure, embraced but unencumbered, free to float through the space."

In this residence, elements of nature provide a spiritual feeling. Water is especially important, with expansive lake views from enormous windows designed to line the back rooms. A world of private serenity where one can witness the sunset and sunrise and fully view the lake's splendor—these rooms define the term "poetry for the soul."

The designers incorporated many items collected from their Asian travels into the architecture so that they look like art commissioned specifically for this home. Japanese and Chinese elements include kimono, antique paintings and drawings and hand-painted screens, all of which accent the tranquility of the overall environment. Geometric shapes and angles conform to the natural surroundings, creating a unity between the man-made structure and the environment.

sacred harbors

palace
in the sky

Southern
California

photography by
© David Glomb

For more than 40 years, the owner of this residence has been enchanted by Morocco. Its exotic smells, tastes and mysteries have captured his heart. So when he asked **John Hutson** to design his California residence, he requested that Hutson use the trove of splendors he had gathered from souks and palaces in Tangier, Fez, Marrakech and Taroudant. Today, these treasured objects transform the penthouse, creating a feeling of heaven on earth for its owner.

No fake arches or Hollywood Moroccan embellishments here. Hutson left the interior volume, with a 20-foot-high ceiling, pristine. It is his arrangement of his client's pieces—from the Ottoman Empire, 18th-century Egypt and Syria—that breaks up the large space into intimate areas, creating the feeling of a many-roomed Moroccan palace. The long corridor area becomes a fantasy souk. Lanterns from Tangier guide guests past a set of hand-painted antique doors from Fez to the grand salon with its myriad of carefully displayed artifacts.

"Best of all, the owner says nothing is too precious to touch," says Hutson. "He encourages guests to rub the amber together until it releases its pungent smell, to play with the elephants' dangling jewels, and wash with the ever-present rose water.

"Primarily, he hopes they will see what he sees. To him, as to the master craftsmen who made these things, these possessions are but expressions of faith in God, showing the interconnectedness of all living things. The pattern work—cascading unbroken lines and intricate beauties—fascinates even the uninitiated."

In the entry hall, Hutson designed a wall of mirrors, increasing the play of light from the Moroccan lanterns. Hand-painted antique doors from Fez define the turn in the hall. ✧ The mother-of-pearl mirror is Ottoman Empire, 16th century, while the armoire and kursy are from Syria, 19th-century. The mother-of-pearl chair with arms is flat backed to cast no shadows, as this could suggest volume as forbidden in the Koran. ✧ The 11-foot tall armoire is rare because it has two doors rather than one. Beyond, a mirror from the Ottoman Empire reflects candelabra from Tangier.

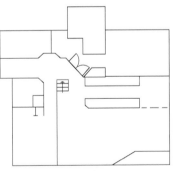

first floor

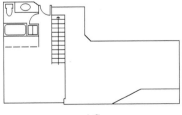

second floor

Cargo Art artist and anthropologist **Sarah Keene Meltzoff** creates a fusion of ancestor spirits from tribal villages and nature with the souls of industrial society. Combining old tools and machine parts with bits of bridewealth, fetishes and nature collected during fieldwork, she bonds the power of the ancestors to the strength of the machine world in order to attract wealth, happiness and love. Her Cargo Art is full of friendly characters who make people smile. As Meltzoff says, "Animated and humorous, they visually interface with antiques and modern design since they themselves are the marriage of two worlds."

Cargo Art plays off tribal art's visual motifs. Meltzoff, who has studied and taught tribal art for years, explains: "Cargo Art is a road to reunifying art, technology and spirituality in our fragmented society."

The 1926 Mediterranean-style house retains its original wooden windows and floors, Pecky cyprus beams, wrought iron chandeliers and detailed fireplace. It has its own persona. There is a vibrant atmosphere created by the saturated colors of the Italian lime-based paints that surround the Moroccan rugs, Bolivian mantas, Panamanian molas and Portuguese quilting with Cargo Art.

Composer Bruce Lazarus fills the spaces with his harpsichord music. A handwritten score of his concerto in a special box frame hangs opposite their bed. They have cultivated a jungle with exotic fruits and flowers. The garden acts as a curtain, angling sunlight into the house in warm and playful ways. They call the house and its garden "Fanalei," after one Solomon Islands village where she has done fieldwork.

cargo art
spirits

Miami
Florida

photography by
Lanny Provo

The garden's light angles natural illumination into the home, creating a play of shadows with Meltzoff's Cargo Art and the original 1926 architectural details of the revered Edwin Corbelli. ❖ Peering down from Meltzoff's Cargo Art studio and showroom are *Fascinated by Manners, The Spirits Have to be Recognized to Become Real, Fishing Charm, Entering the Age of Play, Mask to Advertize Emotion,* and their friends. ❖ The living room's turmeric yellow hue looks into the papaya red of the writing room. At the left is a brightly painted 1800s wooden altar from the Philippines flanked by *One Should Worship a Dog by Becoming Oneself a Dog* and *Seaspirit Master.* On the right, guarding the entrance into the writing room, are *Nightjar Moon* (long-handled Argentinean flat brass spoon, bird skull and tail feathers from a chuck-will's-widow of the Nightjar family), the Naga clan mother, and San Miguel slaying the devil. ❖ Above the bed, with his beard of jungle rope, *I Have Met the Eyes of My Native Companions* surveys the scene. Erzulie, Haitian spirit of love, faces the bed enveloped in a Tanzanian mosquito net. The altar on the dresser reveres a pair of old Javanese mosquito net holders for a wedding bed.

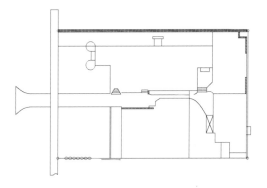

star temple

Santa Fe
New Mexico

photography by
Lynn Lown

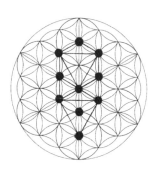

When **James Jereb, Ph.D.** moved to Santa Fe, he became aware of the relationship between design in North Africa and New Mexico—particularly in adobe structures. Soon, this Orientalist and expert on North Africa began merging elements of the two cultures in his own exuberantly colorful and mystical designs.

In early 1996, his life took a totally different direction. He had a vision of an Indian guide named Grandfather that changed his life forever. The instructions from the spirit were simple—create a sacred space to act as a Star Temple and surrender to the Creative Source. Jereb's Light Warrior Studio, where he lives, creates and sees clients, is a place in which to create murals, paintings on canvas, and star gates.

More recently, Jereb has begun channeling. He has become a medium for the archangel Raphael. Raphael told him that the basis of the design of this space would be grounded in the Kabbalah—the grid of the ancients and the Tree of Life ritual. The grid of 10 positions, called Sephiroth, and the 22 paths of movement would change the energy of the space and induce altered states of consciousness for healing and meditation.

Somewhat perplexed by the magnitude of it all, Jereb trusted and surrendered to the process. The result, 22 paintings that he believes are channeled from the Divine, are displayed in his Star Temple. They act as holographic portraits that evoke the multi-dimensional selves in all of us.

"The star gate paintings act as portals into the ancient knowledge and healing traditions of the stars from various indigenous and ancient cultures around the globe," he says.

The altar is the first position, or crown, of the Kabbalah's Tree of Life. An altar within an altar, it includes a statue of Ganesh from India and an altar of Hopi star kachinas. 10-foot-tall cactus mark positions 2, 3, 4, 5, 7, 8 in the Kabbalah's Tree of Life design on which Star Temple is based. The sixth position, Tiphareth, or heart, is marked by an incense table that has an altar of Zuni stone fetishes representing the prophecy of the merging of North and South American traditions. The coffee table is made of an 18th-century door from Morocco.

Jon and Missy Butcher's house is filled, joyously with art, music and nature. Illuminated by lighting designer **Bruce Yarnell**, following nature's best examples, it celebrates life, health and creativity.

Both Butchers sing and produce their own compact disks. He is a fine artist. They exercise religiously and eat healthfully. Their ritual of walking together daily in their Japanese garden is sacrosanct. So are their friends—when they arrive at the front door, no doorbell sounds. Instead, glass doors slide noiselessly open. When guests step inside, they are bathed in an amber pool of cleansing light, an invitation to leave their cares behind.

"I concentrated on five themes—light, fire, water, plants and artwork," says Jon, whose intimate involvement in the design process included covering the walls with sand-painted butcher paper he made with his brother-in-law.

Those five themes are everywhere. Two gigantic fireplaces at the center of the great room, the heart of the house, emanate warmth and symbolize love. The property also includes five waterfalls, indoor and outdoor swimming pools, and interior water features. The family more often than not dines under trees in the living room. Provocative works of art abound, including pieces by Jenny Holzer, Sigmar Polke, Cindy Sherman, Chuck Arnoldi, Chakia Booker, John Chamberlain and Andy Warhol. Each is illuminated by Yarnell with crisp, white gallery-quality lighting.

All else in this light-filled oasis is colored, warmed and textured by Yarnell's deft use of an array of lamps, filters and fixtures. He has produced a kaleidoscope of effects that energize mind, body and soul.

light-filled
oasis

St. Charles
Illinois

photography by
© Michael Spillers 1997

Projected patterns of leaves highlight the way to the exercise and audio-visual rooms. ◇ Guests walk through sliding entry doors to a pool of amber light, making them look instantly more healthy—and hopefully feeling healthier, too. A granite bench from Jenny Holzer's Truisms series is engraved with sayings including, "Selflessness is the highest achievement." ◇ The dining room, which doubles as a library, has two round tables rather than one long formal one. The painting by Chicago's Zhou brothers, is oil and acrylic on canvas and titled Man and Nature.

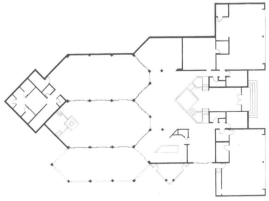

transcending
borders

Coronado
California

photography by
Mary E. Nichols

Part whimsy. Part magic. Part reality. John and Marcia Price's collection of Mexican art is so colorful, imaginative and emotionally charged that it demands a home to match.

Of course, finishes and furnishings can't possibly repeat the explosive colors of artists, such as Bustamente and Jimenez without visually igniting another Mexican revolution. But an imaginative design can capture the essence of the civilization from which the art springs.

"The key was to not compete with the art but to give it a backdrop," explains designer **Charlotte S. Jensen.** She gutted the Prices' vacation home, then grounded it in thick plaster walls, vega log ceilings and Mexican paver tiles. Although the residence is located in a high-rise condominium building, it's hard to believe it is not actually rooted in Mexican soil. That, of course, is just what the Prices wanted.

"Coronado is so close to the Mexican border that I wanted to blend its culture into our living environment," says Marcia Price, a nationally active art advocate.

The collection she wanted installed in this home is a transcultural mix. It includes—along with Mexican works—Native American baskets and art by a variety of U.S. artists similar in spirit to their Mexican counterparts. Jensen had a monumental task just to organize it. Some pieces required hanging. Others needed formal display elements. Still others were placed close at hand. Furthermore, every item had to be illuminated properly. The final result expresses visually what Jensen's client fervently believes. Comments Price, "Art can transcend borders. It is one of the best ways to bring two cultures together. It empowers our lives."

In the entry hall, vega logs are placed in recesses between the soffits, the light filtering down like sunlight through an outdoor Mexican arbor. ✧ An off-white background for walls and upholstery complements the collection's vivid primary colors. The beaded jaguar heads are by Indians in Puerto Vallarta. The opaque acrylic sculpture is by Vassarely. ✧ A rug from Turkey and pillow fabric from Guatemala punctuate the sea of heavily-textured cotton upholstery along with the bronze coffee table sculpted by Sergio Bustamante. Its glass top provides a setting for Eve by Pilar Probil and marble apples by Gregory St. Thomas. ✧ Thick walls abundant with illuminated niches to display the Gregory St. Thomas Mexican-inspired figurines transform the master dressing area.

benevolent voodoo

Coconut Grove
Florida

photography by
Lanny Provo
Horst Neumann

In the home of interior designer **Dennis Jenkins** and tile merchant Sunny McLean, reality is experienced on many levels. For years, Jenkins and McLean have worked on the structure, assembling, sculpturing, painting, willing their artful fantasies into tangible realities. Every aspect of the house speaks to the importance of allowing art to infuse every aspect of life.

The latest addition to this haven of casual privacy is a voodoo shrine Jenkins has constructed from pieces of Sarah Keene Meltzoff's Cargo Art collection. "By making a shrine, the individual attempts to pay homage to the idea of seeking knowledge beyond what is commonly known," says Jenkins. "To become one with the dance of life...to dance within the dance...to be part of the very texture of natural harmonies, because nature is everything and everywhere."

Jenkins views nature as a prime element of reality. He uses his home as a canvas to constantly express this. Moreover, he dances with it, choreographing every element of his environment: layers on layers of painting, tile worked and reworked, an effusion of art and artifacts. Art is not just displayed. It is embedded into walls, which themselves have been sculpted by hand. In every space, the site's surrounding nature is invited to course through, reflecting his belief that one feels natural harmonies without precisely defining them.

"When I sculpture space—when I constructed the shrine—I know what I am doing is important, but I don't know why," he concludes. "I learn from the process. It gives me a reason to keep designing."

Broken ceramic and terracotta tiles, an abstraction of native Seminole fabric design, provide a mystical reference in an atrium area, while the ceiling of glass totally ties the space to the surrounding nature. ◇ Terra cotta and French blue ceramic tile around a hand-carved teaching tablet from the Euphrates brings a feeling of history and a sense of things unknown to the library/bathroom. ◇ An altar made from Sarah Keene Meltzoff's Cargo Art provides the latest addition to this home ◇ In the master bedroom, Miami artist Ellen Moss rendered the designer's ideas of tropical symbolism with benevolent Haitian voodoo symbols.

Two hundred and fifty years ago, pilgrims passed through this portal seeking shelter in a seaside inn. This vaulted interior faced with rough-hewn stone and plaster provided the first resting place in the Holy Land for travellers to Jerusalem.

Today, in the restored ancient citadel of Jaffa, the city's first Jewish hostel has been transfigured by the vision of one artist into a sanctuary of a different kind. **Ilana Goor**, internationally renowned artist, designer and sculptress, has created in this space an odyssey of the soaring spirit. Working with architect **Eran Jacoby**, she transformed the ancient hostel into her own home, which also serves as the museum she founded with her husband Leonard Lowengrub.

Ilana Goor's life's work graces the complex of rooms. Sculptures, jewelry, furniture created from wood, glass, bronze and iron are intermixed with the etchings, paintings, castings and carvings she has gathered from around the globe.

These magical spaces display Goor's collection of furnishings, which run the gamut of style and period. The rooms also vibrate with the energy of young artists, whose work Goor exhibits.

Throughout, the enormity of what Goor has achieved serves as homage to this legendary site. Here, according to myth, Andromeda was chained to a rock until rescued by Perseus. Here, the Bible tells us, Jonah emerged after his encounter with the Whale. Here, Richard the Lion-Hearted and Napoleon passed with their legions. And here Saint Peter was born. The azure sky over Jaffa silhouettes its ancient synagogue, minarets and church spires still.

sanctuary of a
different kind

Jaffa
Israel

photography by
Ami Idan

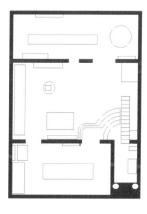

The house/museum's entry is through an open courtyard, its original rough-hewn golden stone providing an interesting contrast to the iron and glass coffee table by Ilana Goor. On the wall beyond is Yaakov Dorchin's The Maiden and Death (1995), constructed of pieces of steel collected from old vehicles. The ceiling is painted blue in the manner of Arabic balances that were said to protect horses from evil. The fireplace, designed by Ilana Goor, was built by Arabs from Bethlehem.

nurturing spaces

casa
polzoni

Rome
Italy

photography by
Claudio Santini

Ancient materials evoking memories and sage wisdom, soaring spaces unified into one harmonious whole: for a couple deeply involved with the arts, these ingredients spell pure bliss.

Located in a central area of Rome not far from the Vatican, yet secluded by gardens from noise, wind and passers-by, the Polzoni residence is an independent annex to a multi-floor apartment complex. Renovated by architect **Angelo Luigi Tartaglia**, the eighth-century stable that contains the Polzoni home encloses a nearly double-height volume with exposed original wooden beams. Tartaglia has reconfigured the space in a nuclear arrangement, with kitchen and bathroom occupying one corner of the great room and the night area above reachable via a wooden staircase. The rest—uplifted by Tartaglia's clean-lined and almost monochromatic furnishings—is left open for inspiration.

The original chestnut beams, soar over ash wood and comfortably upholstered furnishings placed sparingly on natural stone flooring. The entirety is illuminated naturally by day via Tartaglia's design of amply wide windows and balcony doors. At night, recessed wall lights and floor lamps create a warm glow. An expanse of white walls and clear space welcomes a play of light and shadow that seems to dance in unison with the creative aspirations within.

Says Tartaglia, "Every residence should contain within itself the sensibility of the persons who live there. Like a second skin, it must be integrated with their own personalities...to communicate to others their identity and aims, and, more important, so that they themselves can feel comfortable when at home."

The apartment is annexed to a multi-floor apartment building, its façade harmonious with its location in Rome not far from the Vatican. ◇ Loft spaces configured around the central living space provide a sense of communion with the entire environment. ◇ Chairs designed by Charles Eames emphasize the clients' desire for a pared down, creative environment unfettered by anything but essentials. ◇ As in the surrounding exterior garden, the natural materials and history go hand-in-hand with the inhabitants' aesthetic sense.

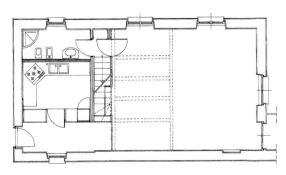

a respect for nature

Los Gatos
California

photography by
Alan Weintraub

Located atop a ridge in the Santa Cruz Mountains looking west toward the Pacific Ocean, this 1970s home has been remodeled by architect **Peter H. Duxbury** and interior designer **Glenda Martin** to protect its privacy from an adjacent residence and make it more integral to the site. Above all, they have expressed the location's immense sense of spirituality.

"The thought was to capture the endless vista from the deck and to connect it spiritually with nature without and within," says Duxbury, whose minimalist approach incorporated only natural materials—slate and limestone, natural woods including oak, cedar and fir. The open deck consists of two tiers topped with a honed and rock-faced limestone bench. A secondary deck with handrail is located below the main deck, leaving the main deck's view unobstructed save for the structure's natural limestone edge.

For the interiors, the forms remain simple as well, focusing on the essential elements of stone, metal, wood, water and fire. Stone is worked throughout by the linear limestone bench, the rough limestone mantel and, in some areas, slate flooring. The fireplace is cleanly expressed by a rectangular void in the featured art wall. Metal is present in the stainless steel cables of the guardrail and the steel guardrail, as well as a fountain at the entry. The sound from its continuous stream of water, which symbolizes the continuity of nature, filters out unwanted noise. The deck, exposed cedar beams and wood floor tie the house to the forested landscape beyond.

A hardwood deck works as a long gallery leading to the entry. With its guard rail illuminated at night, it creates the feeling of a long walk to paradise. Simplicity of line and materials maintains the view's serenity. ◇ By using only white, beige and black in the interior, Peter H. Duxbury and Glenda Martin ensured that nature would provide the only vivid hues. The total neutral color palette, even in the works of art, continues to emphasize the ode to nature expressed through the architecture.

streamlined unity

Gold Coast
Queensland
Australia

photography by
David Knell

The moment the owners decided to build this new home on Queensland's Gold Coast, they knew that the view over the Nerang River and Australia's subtropical climate would make their constant stream of visitors want to spend most of their hours outside. They commissioned landscape architect **Donald Monger**, The Landmark Group, to develop plans for the garden and swimming pool before the house came off their architect's drawing board.

The architect had designed a dramatically contemporary house. Because Monger believes in totally integrating architecture and landscape, he decided to extend the house's characteristic lines to the garden. The shape of the pool and the movement of water—flowing from the upper level down to the swimming pool and then, with the aid of a continuous wet edge, seemingly into the river—dominates the landscape with an equally serendipitous form.

Monger also influenced the architecture of the house, a large structure on three blocks of land that tended to dominate the landscape. To create a greater sense of unity between structure and site, he raised the levels immediately around the house with planter boxes, thus bringing the landscape right into the structure. He increased the size of the planned balconies and extended them in large curving greenscapes out toward the pool, further erasing the distinction between house and garden. He also designed protective glass along the balconies' edges, fitting it into the concrete and thereby eliminating the need for a railing.

"Landscape design that only addresses the garden and fails to speak to the architecture misses that important sense of oneness between people's lives and nature," notes Monger.

Bordered by planter boxes, the balconies do not require hand rails, which would have created an unnecessary feeling of separation between house and garden. Gentle curves of pool and hardscape encourage a sense of movement with no abrupt visual breaks or angles that stop the eye from connecting various aspects of the layered landscape. The swimming pool with its infinity water line appears to be part of the river.

It is not surprising to learn that the reason **James Mary O'Connor** and **Sue O'Brien** moved to Southern California some 12 years ago was O'Connor's opportunity to study and work under the late Charles W. Moore. The architecture of the inspirational Moore is marked by a buoyancy that joyfully celebrates the human spirit. A similar lyrical optimism can be seen today in the work of O'Connor and O'Brien, both architects and husband and wife. Like Moore, they use color as one of their primary tools for expressing this profound spiritual connectedness.

Their own house is characterized by the warm yellow of its exterior. The interior is both open and intimate—an ode to the quality of life they sought for their personal environment. Turning a 625-square-foot 1940s bungalow into a family home and guest apartment of 2,600 square feet, they created an eclectic environment defined by color, space and light to evoke places as far afield as Mexico and Japan.

A subtle unity can be found in some of the long vistas that express the architects' sensibilities about space and color. It is these two features that most distinguish the house. Light and color are used throughout to enliven space. In addition to the work of Moore, the influence of Tina Beebe and Luis Barragan can also be seen here. On a more global scale, O'Connor and O'Brien take visual inspiration from California, Mexico and Japan.

Late at night, the colors glow like an illuminated box of jewels. One is conscious of a special, private enclave that works on every level for this California family.

lyrical
relationships

Santa Monica
California

photography by
Douglas Hill

The living room evokes the feeling of calm island. Its changing planes and north-south orientation shifts from entry to rear garden. Low furniture, the detached fireplace, thick walls enhanced with colors evoking Luis Barragan's San Christobel Stables, and vertical niches create the sensation of height and serenity. ◇ The dining room, which is attached to the kitchen, is a large easy space with high ceilings and streams of natural light from east and west. The staircase, in aquamarine and cobalt blue, leads to the master suite and study. The alcove's unusually shaped rear wall is defined by the same strong mustard yellow used on one of the master bedroom's walls. In the master bedroom, walls painted hyacinth and mustard contrast with the light maple furniture.

first floor

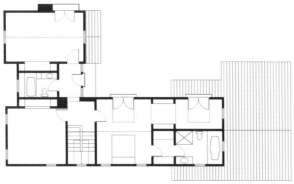

second floor

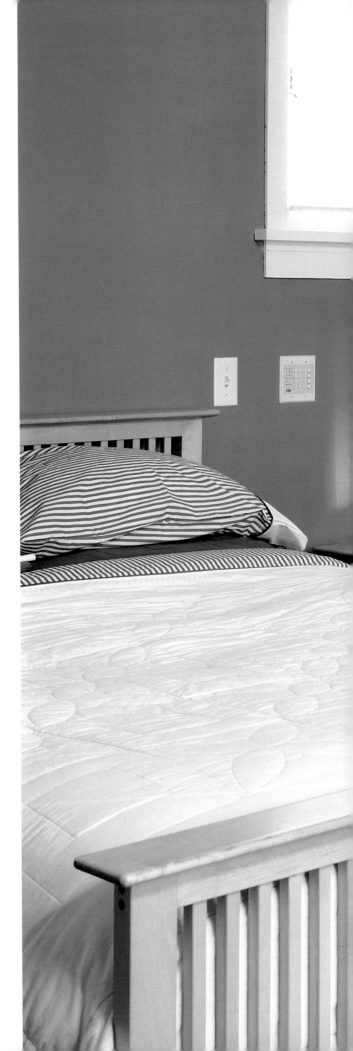

transitions

Mexico City
Mexico

photography by
Arturo Zavala Häag

Do empty walls and the feeling of limitless space free the mind and set it soaring? Architect **José de Yturbe** thinks so. He designed this house with the Japanese concept of wabi (voluntary poverty) in mind, as well as elements of Islamic and pre-Columbian architecture. Voluntary poverty, less is more, lack of ornamentation, concealment of structure within walls to create a serenely flowing integration of nature with interior spaces: These ideas establish the serenity of this residence.

Located in a residential suburb on the west side of Mexico City, the house sits between two steep ravines. While the luxuriant vegetation provides a natural haven from the neighboring properties, the primary architectural challenge was nevertheless to build a quiet refuge from the urban hustle and bustle. Thus the design of the house projects around a central courtyard, drawing the energy inward to the core.

The ritual of transition, the most important aspect of de Yturbe's design philosophy, reveals itself in the progression of spaces. Areas exist solely to lead occupants from one place to another. Similarly, scale, proportion, color and texture are devices used to individualize experience and to pay homage to its every aspect. Entering, gathering, dining and contemplation—each activity is treated as sacred. The use of natural light through an abundance of windows and skylights marks the progress of time and its various moods, paying tribute to each moment of each day.

Architecture that so connects the individual to the essence of life by removing all but the fundamentals answers the question before it is asked.

The house projects around a central courtyard. Elements of Islamic design typically found in the Iberian peninsula—such as the use of water for both its acoustical and ornamental properties—are reflected in the landscape of the courtyard's open volume. ◇ Designed for a family with four teenage children, the home's great room provides for study, multimedia experiences, and family gatherings amid a harmonious circumference. Color and light are intimately related throughout the house to emphasize emotion. A yellow-painted lattice creates a joyful play of light and shadow.

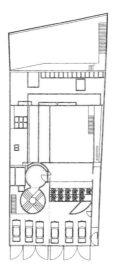

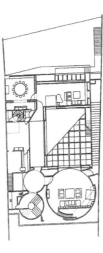

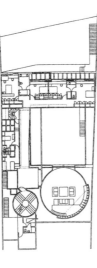

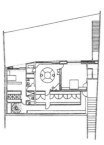

To architect **David Kellen**, the idea of design's spiritual influence has been his interest as long as he can remember. When he launched into his architectural career, it became increasingly clear to him that one of the most important functions of architecture was its effect on the human soul. An example is this home he designed. While comforting and protective, it also celebrates the idea of home as heightened awareness of the connection of the everyday to the spiritual. To make his point, Kellen uses several tactics to catch the viewer off-guard and thus more likely engage in Kellen's spiritual perspective.

The presence of the pool house forms a surreal and somewhat dream-like composition—"Surrealism in art always being one of the gateways to the spiritual world," notes Kellen. "And remember, the spiritual world never is as heavy and grounded as the physical world."

The architecture's extremely vertical presence suggests another emotional state that links the spiritual world with the physical. Also, adds Kellen, "Exterior materials are brought into the design to break down the notion of what is interior space and what is exterior. Anything that interrupts what the user takes for granted can switch him on to seeing the physical world differently and linking him to things more spiritual."

inspired
gateway

Beverly Hills
California

photography by
Ross Rappaport

Shifting angles and floating planes emulate the free-flowing dynamics of a spiritual state. The entry is intensely vertical in scale and direction, allowing the stair to dance to the second floor. The heaviness of the terrazzo floor below is juxtaposed with the mystery of hidden indirect lighting and partially hidden skylights above. Integral to the design is a gallery for the owner's collection of surreal art and custom designed furniture. ◊ The furniture, including the table designed and fabricated by Kellen, supports the strong play of the rectilinear geometries and thus the idea of the physical world in contrast to the dynamic movement of the natural, spiritual world.

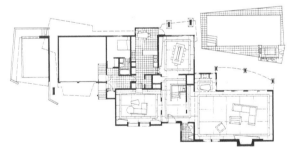

first floor

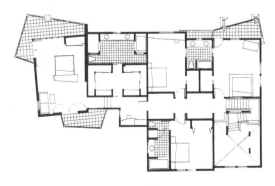

second floor

To architects **Polly Osborne** and **John Erickson** and associate **Carol Hove**, designing is itself a spiritual work.

"The singular silence that a beautiful building emits is, for me, the highest spiritual experience," says Polly.

With Osborne Erickson Architects, attitude is everything. Finding the link that unifies structure and site with the people who live there—and then following through with each detail—they consciously strive in each space they design to instill the greatest degree of sensitivity possible. The renovation of this 1925 Mediterranean residence for David and Sherril Anderle is an undeniable expression of the harmony among the individuals involved.

All were in agreement about keeping the house's original footprint. The designers re-proportioned exterior and interior spaces and redefined certain areas to create a new den and bath. Everyone understood the lasting emotional and aesthetic benefits that resulted from the architects going beyond mere ornament to incorporate the work ethic into this residence. Osborne, Erickson and Hove took the extra steps to perfect every detail: working side-by-side with contractors and crew, they hand-carved drawer pulls and designed special tiles for continuity of pattern.

Downstairs, they played with the existing structures and styles. Upstairs, they played against them. For example, in the first floor den saturated colors, bird's-eye maple and cherry wood create a tour de force of the craftsman aesthetic. Yet the master suite above departs dramatically, with large expanses of pale fabrics and birch wood highlighted by abundant natural light.

Above all, there was no dissension. This can be felt as well as seen.

singular
harmony

Los Angeles
California

photography by
Derek Rath

The formerly uninviting, dark living room is now a favorite spot because of comfortable furniture and stained-glass windows reconfigured to let in more light. The portraits of Bob Dylan and Brian Wilson were painted by David Anderle, a music-industry executive. ◇ Custom-designed furnishings in the master bedroom include an audio-visual cabinet, dressing screen, bed and side tables. All are made of light birch wood with black accents, providing this long and spacious room with a cohesive look.

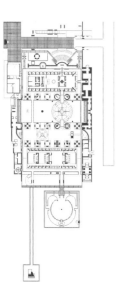

inspired
journey

Sea Island
Georgia

photography by
Michael Portman

John Portman designed his house museum Entelechy II in the early 1980s. Throughout the year, he and his wife Jan use it as a weekend retreat. In the summer, it serves as a beach house for the Portman's multigenerational family.

The house is large—12,586 square feet of enclosed space with more than 7,000 square feet of decks and patios. More impressive than its size is the way structure and nature integrate. Portman has also used art within and without to make it truly the serene place that he envisioned: he spends a great deal of time there in reflection.

"Its attempt to understand its place and era is infused with man as human and spiritual—an integral part of the natural and man-made world," he says of this home. "It is an effort not only to express but to create a small haven to inspire one's journey within the continued search of meaning."

The footprint is established by the rectangular sunscreen, which unifies and shelters four pavilions constructed on a grid created by 18 massive "exploded" columns. The pavilions provide zones for more intimate activity within the context of the grand and spacious home.

Directly facing the Atlantic Ocean, Entelechy II is the second Portman residence named after Aristotle's term for that which makes actual what is otherwise merely potential. The house is "of the sea" in concept and detailing. The architectural concept grew from the form of the beach umbrella that provides shade and shelter without blocking the sea breeze. The house does likewise, pulled apart vertically and horizontally to allow breezes to gently flow throughout.

Says Portman, "The essence of Entelechy II is architecture as sculpture—sculpture begetting sculpture—yet pragmatic as to function and livability with its dichotomy of form and space defining each other." Art enriches the experience of each space. In the living-dining room, John Portman's Organica (1983) (far right) is joined by Neptune's Helmet by Stephanie Scuris on the coffee table, a wood composition by Ghysels Upward Ritual (maquette) on the end table, and Black Boxes by Beppe Giuliani on the back wall. The painting is Mire G 109 "Kowloon" by Jean Dubuffet. On the table is a sculpture by Hans Frabel.

art,
nature,
friends

Northern Italy

photography by
Gionata Xerra

Since there is nothing more captivating than happiness and love, there was no way that Milanese architects **Antonio Citterio** and **Terry Dwan** could refuse the married couple who asked them to design their new house—even though its foundation had already been completed. While the designers couldn't start from scratch, they could respond to the clients' desire for an inviting, open environment. This house, which overlooks a lake, is devoted to its occupants' favorite pastimes—art, nature, friends and each other.

Although the building size was almost completely defined, Citterio and Dwan were able to bring in much more natural light and even extend the space outward toward the expansive patio. Indeed, they have turned the entire home into what feels like one harmonious white-washed indoor-outdoor area. It is ideal for relaxing and viewing art. Its floor-to-ceiling window wall turns the site's abundant greenery into another huge canvas.

The 10,000-square-foot house sits on three levels. The ground floor is entirely dedicated to art and social life. The first floor is devoted to the private dimension of the clients' life and includes a studio as well as bedroom and bathroom. The oak-paneled basement, while partially closed and thereby suitable for meditation and sauna, includes its own light-filled patio centered around a tree. It is in this basement area that the architects also included room for billiards, an expansive living room with fireplace, a wine cellar and a secondary kitchen complete with built-in oven for cooking pizza and bread.

All areas are characterized by the same materials. The smooth plaster walls are painted white to emphasize the art and scenery. Oak combined with a Vicenza stone is used for the flooring that continues outdoors and completely encircles the residence—creating a total envelope of uninterrupted serenity. For interest and function, the composition is broken by a few perpendicular lines that move from the structure's core and mark principal pathways.

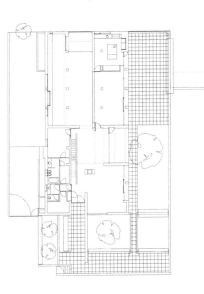

"The idea," says interior designer **Arthur Porras**, "was for the home I designed with architect **Ken Ronchetti** to embody a continuity of concept—to meld site, architectural form and interior into one." Porras wanted to capture the sea, in all its vastness, within the residence of Mr. and Mrs. James Clarke.

The elements of the Pacific Ocean—its cliffs and its tides—resonate with natural forces. Porras has harnessed them to meet here in a moment of peace. It is as if movement and sound cease—each element in the home becomes a symbolic representation of both. The fireplace is at once curvilinear and rectangular. Soft fabrics play against hard surfaces. The pool ascending from the ocean echoes its mystery, transposing both fluid calm and humbling force to the house. These contextual rhythms are repeated throughout, reverberating harmonies of texture, color and line.

"That river is within me and all that surrounds me, as the river flowing beneath a river imparts a spirit to be sensed intuitively," comments Porras.

"Space, like silence, is a continuous presence defined only by interruption," he continues. "The careful balance of opposing forms and shapes achieves a sense of tranquility and oneness—the contrast of surfaces and materials, curvilinear elements juxtaposed to rectangular elements, the positive forms defined by their negative forms."

All is held together within a neutrally hued background. Taking the colors from the site's cliffs and sand and moving them through the spectrum, they reflect changing hues with each day's progression and ground the variety of textures and materials. The accent of color defines space, as does the ocean outside.

resonant
forces

La Jolla
California

photography by
Mary E. Nichols

Rhythms emanating from the sea ascend to the structure in comforting waves of form. ❖ The dining room includes a series of metaphors—the circle symbolizing the universe, the square a symbol of the earth. ❖ A balance of opposites creates harmony in the living room: the fireplace at once curvilinear and rectangular; the soft fabrics juxtaposed with stucco, concrete and stone; forms piercing negative space. ❖ A stairway ascends to the upper level's private living area—a contextual rhythm repeating visually the cadence of ocean waves pounding outside.In the lower level barroom, a subtle palette of natural textures and colors creates harmony. ❖ The total effect is a circle within a square within a circle within a square, held together with color and texture.

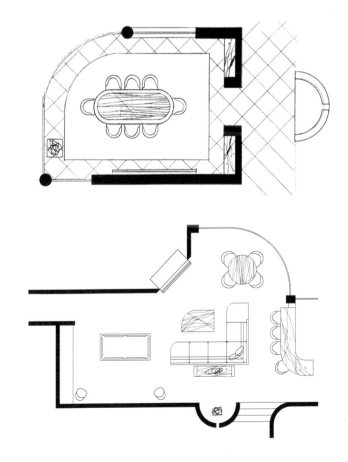

directory

architects & interior designers

Angelo Luigi Tartaglia, Architetto
Via Boezio 92 D9a
Rome 00192 Italy
tel: 39 06 687 3879
fax: 39 06 686 8449
e-mail: tartaglia@tiscalinet.it

Antonio Citterio & Partners
Via Lovanio 8
Milaan 20121 Italy
tel: 39 02 655 59 02
fax: 39 02 655 13 03
e-mail: citterio@mdsnet.it

Architectural Artworks Incorporated
163 East Morse Boulevard
Winter Park, Florida 32789
tel: 407 644 1410
fax: 407 644 1016
e-mail: info@arch-art.com

Art + Design
2400 Lytton Springs Road
Healdsburg, California 95448
tel: 415 922 7855
fax: 415 922 7861
e-mail: toglenda@mindspring.com

Arthur Porras ASID & Associates
611 West G Street Suite 122
San Diego, California 92101
tel: 619 702 2298
fax: 619 702 7611

Bron Design Group
PO Box 32115
Phoenix, Arizona 85016
tel: 602 955 1053
fax: 602 957 4154
e-mail: bron_design@earthlink.net

Charlotte Jensen & Associates
11464 Escoba Place
San Diego, California 92127
tel: 858 693 9294
fax: 858 487 6895

Créations Pietro Seminelli
171 rue du Faubourg Saint Antoine
Paris 75011 France
tel: 33 01 4347 4411
fax: 33 01 4347 4415
e-mail: pietrosem@aol.com

David Kellen + Associates, Inc.
3200 Airport Avenue #10
Santa Monica, California 90405
tel: 310 313 2199
fax: 310 313 4250
e-mail: dkellen@earthlink.net
website: davidkellenassociates.com

Dennis Jenkins & Associates
5813 Southwest 68th Street
South Miami, Florida 33143
tel: 305 665 6960
fax: 305 665 6971
e-mail: design424@aol.com

de Yturbe Arquitectos
Sierra Mojada 262-2
Lomas de Barrilaco
Mexico DF 11010 Mexico
tel: 525 540 4368
fax: 525 520 8621
e-mail: deyturbe@infosel.net.mx
website: deyturbe.com

Duxbury Architects
382 A First Street
Los Altos, California 94022
tel: 650 917 3840
fax: 650 917 3848
e-mail: duxarx@aol.com

Geoffrey Bradfield Inc.
105 East 63rd Street
New York, New York 10021
tel: 212 758 1773
fax: 212 688 1571

Geoffrey Scott and Associates
3111 17th Street
Santa Monica, California 90405
tel: 310 396 5416
fax: 310 399 5246
e-mail: gscottasso@aol.com

Glenn Lawson, Inc.
122 East 55th Street 3rd Floor
New York, New York 10022
tel: 212 755 4212
fax: 212 755 4217

Ilana Goor
4 Mazal Dagim #4
Old Jaffa 68036 Israel
tel: 972 03 683 7676
fax: 972 03 683 6699

Jacoby Architects
64 Sokolov Street
Ramat Hasharon 47235 Israel
tel: 972 03 547 0338
fax: 972 03 547 1340
e-mail: eranarc@bereqint.net

Jeffrey Daniels & Associates
8617 Lookout Mountain Avenue
Los Angeles, California 90046
tel: 323 654 3282
fax: 323 654 2308
e-mail: jdaniels@unex.ucla.edu

J. Frank Fitzgibbons AIA, Architect
4822 Glencairn Road
Los Angeles, California 90027
tel: 323 663 7579
fax: 323 663 6262
e-mail: ifitzgibbons@hsc.usc.edu

John Hutson Designs
1932 Calvert Street NW #3
Washington DC 20009
tel: 310 275 5375
fax: 310 247 9285
e-mail: johnhutson1@earthlink.net

John Portman & Associates
303 Peachtree Street NE
Atlanta, Georgia 30308
tel: 404 614 5252
fax: 404 614 5553
e-mail: jpaatl@mindspring.com
website: portmanusa.com

Ken Ronchetti Design Inc.
PO Box 474
Rancho Santa Fe, California 92067
tel: 858 756 1033
fax: 858 756 9669
e-mail: krddlc1@aol.com

The Landmark Group
32/78 Cairns Street
Kangaroo Point Brisbane 4169 Australia
tel: 61 7 3891 1190
fax: 61 7 3891 1598
e-mail: don@landmarkgroup.com.au
website: landmarkgroup.com.au

Legorreta Arquitectos
Palacio de Versalles 285-A
Lomas Reforma Mexico DF 11020 Mexico
tel: 525 251 9698
fax: 525 596 6162
e-mail: legorret@data.net.mx

Light Warrior Foundation
901 West San Mateo Studio R+S
Santa Fe, New Mexico 87505
tel: 505 989 8765
fax: 505 989 3353

Lotus Antiquities
158 North La Brea Avenue
Los Angeles, California 90036
tel: 323 938 4531
fax: 323 938 4731
e-mail: bwblairlotus@earthlink.net

Sarah Keene Meltzoff
152 NE 93rd Street
Miami, Florida 33138
tel: 305 756 5522
fax: 305 361 4675
e-mail: smeltzoff@rsmas.miami.edu

Nakane Garden Research &
Landscape Consultant Corporation
1-6 Karatanouchi-Cho Taniguchi
Ukyo-ku Kyoto 616-8013 Japan
tel: 81 75 465 2373
fax: 81 75 465 2374
e-mail: nakane@lares.dti.ne.jp

O'Connor + O'Brien Design Associates
638 Marine Street
Santa Monica, California 90405
tel: 310 392 4364
fax: 310 396 2239
e-mail: oisino@aol.com

Osborne Erickson Architects
1525 South Sepulveda Boulevard Suite A
Los Angeles, California 90025
tel: 310 477 2855
fax: 310 477 7765
e-mail: posbo@earthlink.net

Pizzinini/Luxemburg
2828 Donald Douglas Loop North
Santa Monica, California 90405
tel: 310 452 9667
fax: 310 452 9697
e-mail: pizzilux@ni.net

Sandra Nunnerley Inc.
595 Madison Avenue Suite 2300
New York, New York 10022
tel: 212 826 0539
fax: 212 826 1146
e-mail: sandra@nunnerly.com

Shubin + Donaldson Architects, Inc.
629 State Street Suite 244
Santa Barbara, California 93101
tel: 805 966 2802
fax: 805 966 3002
e-mail: email@sandarc.com
website: sandarc.com

Sig Bergamin Interiors, Inc.
20 East 69th Street #3C
New York, New York 10021
tel: 212 861 4515
fax: 212 861 3667

Martin John Smyth
Third Floor
94A Pokfulam Road
Hong Kong
tel: 852 2818 9258
fax: 852 2817 9142
e-mail: smyth@iohk.com

Thomas Barrie AIA
Associate Professor
College of Architecture and Design
Lawrence Technological University
2100 West Ten Mile Road
Southfield, Michigan 48075
tel: 248 204 2870
fax: 248 204 2900
e-mail: barrie@liu.edu

Walter Bendix Nelson, Architect
P O Box 4549
Cave Creek, Arizona 85327
tel/fax: 480 595 8618

Yarnell Associates Architectural
Lighting Design
12616 West 71st Street
Shawnee, Kansas 66216
tel: 913 268 9206
fax: 913 268 4468
e-mail: bruce@yarnellassociates.com
website: yarnellassociates.com

photographers

Alan Weintraub Photography
1832 Mason Street
San Francisco, California 94133
tel: 415 553 819
fax: 415 553 8192

Jaime Ardiles-Arces
730 Fifth Avenue 9th Floor
New York, New York 10019
tel: 212 333 8779
fax: 212 593 2070

Assassi Productions
P O Box 3651
Santa Barbara, California 93130
tel: 805 682 2158
fax: 805 682 1185
e-mail: assassi@att.net

Cecile & Stefano Poli
163 rue de Charenton
Paris 75012 France
tel/fax: 33 1 43 45 99 29
e-mail: cspoli@club-internet.fr

David Knell and Associates
3 Banning Street Wishart
Brisbane Queensland 4122 Australia
tel/fax: 61 7 3343 4461

Everett & Soulé
553 East Oakhurst Street
Altamonte Springs, Florida 32701
tel/fax: 407 831 4183
e-mail: asoule@cfl.rr

David Glomb
71340 Estellita Drive
Rancho Mirage, California 92270
tel: 760 340 4455
fax: 760 779 1872

H. Durston Saylor Inc.
101 West 23rd Street Box 2259
New York, New York 10011
tel: 212 779 3901
fax: 973 783 5573
e-mail: thaxton@aol.com

Arturo Zavala Häag
Cafetos 122
Bosques de las Lomas
Mexico DF 11700 Mexico
tel: 525 596 1510
fax: 525 245 0207
e-mail: superturi@hotmail.com

Douglas Hill
2324 Moreno Drive
Los Angeles, California 90039
tel: 323 660 0681
fax: 323 663 8688
e-mail: odouglas@aol.com
website: doughill.com

Hugo A. Rojas Photography
5232 Alhambra Avenue
Los Angeles, California 90032
tel: 323 222 8836
fax: 323 222 5551

Ami Idan
Salame Street 15
Tel Aviv 68111 Israel
tel: 972 3 518 2408
fax: 972 3 518 2407
e-mail: zavitm@zahav.net.il

Michael Janeczek
77 Road Street
Ludlow, Massachusetts 01056
tel/fax: 413 547 0267

Lanny Provo Photography
100 NE 101st Street
Miami Shores, Florida 33138
tel/fax: 305 756 0136

Lourdes Legorreta
Parque via Reforma #1920
Colonia Lomas de Chapultepek
Miguel Hidalgo 11000 Mexico
tel: 525 520 6530
fax: 525 520 6036

Mark Boisclair Photography, Inc.
2512 East Thomas Road #1
Phoenix, Arizona 85016
tel: 602 957 6997
fax: 602 957 8494
e-mail: markbphoto@aol.com

Mary E. Nichols Photography
444 North McCadden Place
Los Angeles, California 90004
tel: 323 930 1926
fax: 323 930 1279
e-mail: marysouth@mindspring.net

Michael Portman Photography
7 Bentley Manor
Atlanta, Georgia 30327
tel: 770 850 0509
fax: 770 956 0225
e-mail: mwpphoto@mindspring.com

Charis Mundy
Flat F Third Floor
Kam Yuen No. 3 Old Peak Road
Hong Kong
tel: 852 2840 1585
fax: 852 2840 1597
e-mail: midgle2@attglobal.net

Nakane Garden Research &
Landscape Consultant Corporation
1-6 Karatanouchi-Cho Taniguchi
Ukyo-ku Kyoto 616-8013 Japan
tel: 81 75 465 2373
fax: 81 75 465 2374
e-mail: nakane@lares.dti.ne.jp

New Media Arts
3304 El Paseo
Santa Fe, New Mexico 87501
tel: 505 820 3177
fax: 505 820 3179
e-mail: info@nmarts.com
website: nmarts.com

Paul Hyman Productions
124 West 79th Street
New York, New York 10024
tel: 212 580 6501
fax: 212 874 5365

Photography for the Built Environment
421 East 69th Terrace
Kansas City, Missouri 64131
tel/fax: 816 444 0882
e-mail: spillers@kcnet.com

Ross Rappaport
730 Palms Avenue
Venice, California 90291
tel: 310 822 8529
fax: 310 306 9719

Rath & Associates
4044 Moore Street
Los Angeles, California 90066
tel/fax: 310 305 1342
e-maill: rathd@earthlink.net

Claudio Santini
12915 Greene Avenue
Los Angeles, California 90066
tel: 310 578 7919
fax: 310 578 9229
e-mail: artcla@aol.com

Studio Horst Neumann Oy
Varastokuja 4
Helsinki 00580 Finland
tel: 358 9 753 0190
fax: 358 9 753 0197
e-mail: horst.neumann@horstneumann.com
website: horstneumann.com

Tom Bonner Photography
1201 Abbot Kinney Boulevard
Venice, California 90291
tel: 310 396 7125
fax: 310 396 4792
e-mail: tsbphoto@aol.com

Toshi Yoshimi Photography
4030 Camero Avenue
Los Angeles, California 90027
tel: 323 660 9043
fax: 323 660 2497
e-mail: tyoshimi@earthlink.net

Tuca Reinés Photography
R. Emanuel Kant 58
São Paulo SP Brazil 04536050
tel: 55 11 3061 9127
fax: 55 11 852 8735

Dominique Vorillon
1636 Silverwood Terrace
Los Angeles, California 90026
tel: 323 660 5883
fax: 323 660 5575

Wade Zimmerman Photography
9 East 97th Street
New York, New York 10029
tel: 212 427 8784
fax: 212 427 3526
e-mail: wzphotos@mciworld.com

Gionata Xerra
Via Carlo Botta 8
Milan 20135 Italy
tel: 39 02 5501 2207
fax: 39 02 5519 5278

special consulants

Taffy Lanser
PO Box 4665
Cave Creek, Arizona 85327
tel: 602 488 0085
fax: 602 595 8288

Taylor & Company
437 North Palm Drive 8
Beverly Hills, California 90210
tel: 310 247 1099
fax: 310 247 8147
e-mail: jtaylorpr@usa.net

Wordwise
5931 Brick Court Suite 130
Winter Park, Florida 32792
tel: 407 657 4818
fax: 407 679 3252
e-mail: wordwisepr@aol.com

acknowledgments

As long as humans have taken shelter, they have imbued it with design and imagery reflective of their aspirations and dreams. Yet today perhaps more than ever there is a profound awakening to the possibilities inherent in good design to not only reflect but participate in the quest for spiritual harmony. I am grateful to be writing at such a time.

In particular it is due to the heartfelt belief of the architects and designers in these pages that what they create connects the individual to the essence of life that led to the development of this volume. Without their understanding and fervor as well as their technical knowledge and skills, this book could not have conveyed the inspiration behind the ideas that now fill its pages.

I am also deeply indebted to PBC International for having the foresight to publish books such as DESIGNING WITH SPIRITUALITY: THE CREATIVE TOUCH and its predecessor, FENG SHUI AT HOME. If, as some predict, the next one hundred years will be the century of spirituality, we are fortunate to become part of it now.

Thank you too to the staff of PBC International for infusing our presentation with the thoughtfulness, taste and precise execution that reflects the high aims and soaring spirit of the subject and its practitioners.

To the esteemed Stanley Abercrombie, my neverending gratitude for continuing to lend your sensitive words to every addition to THE CREATIVE TOUCH series.

Finally, a million bouquets to Barbara Barry for enabling me to interview her for this volume's introduction. Her inspiring perspective on life and design illuminates to an extraordinary degree the book's philosophical basis and author's beliefs.